The Prisons of the Doge's Palace
in Venice

Umberto Franzoi

The Prisons
of the Doge's Palace
in Venice

Electa

www.electaweb.it

Reprint 2004
First edition 1997

Contents

A Historical Tour of the Prisons of the Doge's Palace

In the early years of the ninth century, when Agnello Partecipazio held the office of doge, the communities of the lagoon chose the archipelago of Rivoalto as the site for their activities and the urban space that later came to be known as the area of St. Mark's and is now the location of the Doge's Palace, as their seat of government and the judiciary.

Over the eight centuries that separate the original structure from the one we see today, the Doge's Palace has been enlarged and embellished, renovated and restored innumerable times.

The patricians of Venice chose to house all the institutions of government in the building, including the law courts and the places of punishment and detention.

So right from the start prisons were incorporated in the palace. They were located in the block facing onto the basin and canal until the second half of the sixteenth century, when plans to construct a building on the other side of the canal were put into effect: this was to be used in its entirety as a prison, with rooms set aside for the Magistrati di Notte al Criminal.

At the beginning of the seventeenth century (1602) the new building was connected to the palace by the famous Bridge of Sighs, designed by the architect Antonio Contin.

The Palace Prisons

The whole ground floor of the block facing onto the basin was occupied by a series of prisons. Each group was subdivided into numerous chambers with wooden walls made of crossed and heavily nailed planks. This solution, recorded in a sixteenth-century plan of the ground floor as well, was adopted at the time of the Gothic reconstruction of this part of the palace, begun in 1340 and in all likelihood completed before 1365, when the Paduan painter Guariento was commissioned to fresco the *Coronation of the Virgin* on the wall of the Tribunale in the Sala del Maggior Consiglio.

Yet the prisons had existed even earlier. Documents dated 1297 tell us that the prisons were located not only on the ground floor but also on the floor below the roof. All were unhealthy and provided conditions at the limit of endurance, if not of survival. A detailed estimate for the works to be carried out in the prisons in 1438, drawn up by the curator of the palace, gives a list of all the cells that existed at the

Facing page
The Pozzi: surviving wooden lining of a cell.

The two buildings, separated by the canal, of the Doge's Palace and the Prigioni Nuove. In the foreground the Ponte della Paglia

and in the background the Ponte dei Sospiri, or Bridge of Sighs, which provided a confidential link between the two buildings.

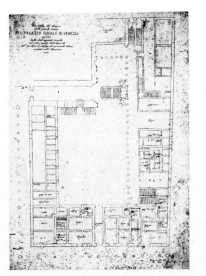

time and their precise names. Starting from the corner on the Piazzetta, we find: the Prigioni delle Donne (women's prisons), Prigioni Nuovissime (new prisons), the Mula, Trona, the Camerotti dei Signori di Notte (chambers of the Lords of Night), and the Malpaga, Liona and Lionessa. Beyond the Porta del Frumento lay the Chiesetta and then the Valiera, the Forte, Mocina, Armamento, Giustiniana, Schiava, Galiota, Fresca Zoia, Gradonia, Catolda (set under the staircase of the censors) and finally the Vulcano. Each of these prisons was subdivided into small cells that opened onto the service corridors. Only part of the rooms were set on two floors, taking up the height of the existing portico.

One of the biggest problems faced by the prison authorities was the overcrowding of these jails, a problem that grew steadily worse

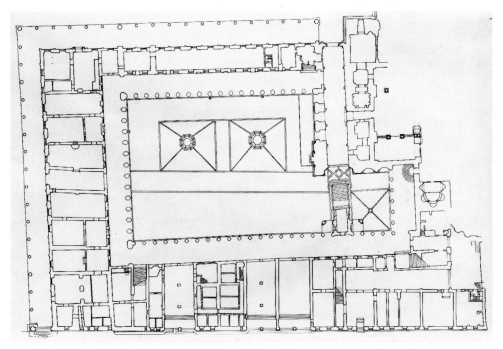

Facing page, top
*The Doge's Palace
and the Prigioni Nuove.*

Bottom
*The Doge's Palace,
front facing the basin.*

*Facsimile of the ground
floor plan of the Doge's
Palace in 1580, made
from the original
inserted in codex CCXCV
class VII of the appendix
to the catalogue of
Italian manuscripts
in St. Mark's Library.*

*Plan of the current
layout of the Doge's
Palace, which dates back
to the early part of the
seventeenth century.
It shows the completion
of the northern
and eastern sides
of the arcade facing onto
the courtyard*

*and the restructuring
of the internal walls
to create larger and more
independent rooms with
windows and doors.*

Old floors, at different
levels, of Istrian stone
and of bricks laid
in a herringbone pattern,
of the prisons
on the ground floor
of the Doge's Palace
on the side facing
the basin.

in the second half of the fifteenth century and over the following two centuries.

The Torresella

The corner tower near the Ponte della Paglia, an ancient vestige of the Doge's Castle, had housed a number of prisons ever since the eleventh century, if not earlier. After 1340 these were reorganized and used, because of their relatively mild conditions, for prisoners of consequence.

From 1460 onward, following several outbreaks of fire in the cells of the Torresella caused by the oil lamps that inmates kept burning day and night, the commitment of prisoners to these cells was decided on each occasion by the Council of Ten.

Twenty-six years later, after the fire in the doge's apartment, the use of the cells was limited to the so-called Forte prison.

Writing on the wall of the cell in the Torresella: "DEUS ... BEATU PETRU APOSTULUS A VINCOLIS ABSOLVIS."

Wall of the last remaining cell in the group of prisons known as Torresella with inscriptions and graffiti. Floor of the armory in the Doge's Palace.

Even today the side wall of this room, on the same floor as the Sala d'Armi, is covered with inscriptions, written or scratched by prisoners at various times.

Pozzi

In January 1531 the Republic resumed work on the palace and reconstructed the building facing onto the canal so that it linked up with the Sala del Maggior Consiglio.

The building provided a worthy home for the first important law courts, from the Council of Ten to the Three Chiefs and the Inquisitors.

In 1525, to remedy the undignified situation that had developed around the jails in the Doge's Palace, it was decided to remove all the prisoners from the cells, which were scattered all over the place and far from functional, and shut them up in the prisons on the ground floor of the fourteenth-century building facing onto the basin.

This was the period in which the overcrowding of the cells reached its highest levels, resulting in numerous cases of illness and death among

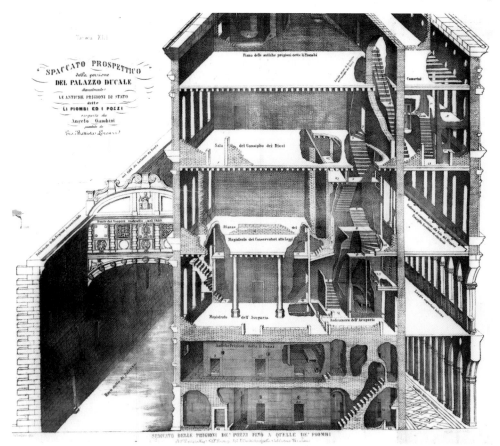

Angelo Gambini, Perspective cutaway of the Doge's Palace showing the former State prisons known as the Piombi and the Pozzi, drawn by Angelo Gambini and owned by Gio. Battista Lorenzi, *engraving, Venice,*

Museo Correr. On the left is shown the Bridge of Sighs and then the side wall of the Prigioni Nuove on the other side of the canal.

*Hall of the Council
of Ten.*

*The Pozzi: inscription
on the vault of a cell.*

Facing page, top left
*The Pozzi: corridor
with cells.*

Facing page, top right
*Passage with movable
shutter of Istrian stone
on the ground floor of the
Pozzi opening onto Riva
Gravenigo.*

Facing page, bottom
*The internal arcade
of the Doge's Palace
onto which the Pozzi
face.*

*One of the flights of steps
that connects two floors
of the Pozzi complex.*

the convicts. An attempt was made to solve these problems by building nine cells under the jurisdiction of the Council of Ten.

Later the same number of cells were created on the mezzanine at the height of the ground-floor portico. These two groups of cells later came to be known as the "Pozzi" (wells or pits) because of their extreme narrowness and discomfort.

All these cells were arranged in a plan in which the patrol corridors ran along the outer walls. The Pozzi were totally independent of the other prisons from the logistical viewpoint and had different, stricter and more selective rules and security measures.

Even the Council of the Ten considered these cells too small, damp and airless, comparing them to "burial places for men."

Piombi

Another group of prisons that are still famous today, called the "Piombi" (Leads), was made up of seven cells located on the floor under the roof. Their name derives from the sheets of lead used to cover the roof. There is a precise reference to the Piombi in a resolution of the Council of Ten passed in 1591. But even in the second half of the fifteenth century there must have already been a number of cells in the attics of the preexisting building that were set aside for the use of the Chiefs of the Council.

Despite the high summer temperatures and cold winters, the Piombi were considered relatively tolerable places of detention and so were assigned to people of account, who had no previous convictions for serious misdeeds or crimes against the State.

The cells had been created by the subdivision of three larger rooms, facing onto the canal and courtyard, by means of wooden partitions again built out of heavily nailed, crossed planks. It was from these prisons that the celebrated Giacomo Casanova made a daring escape in the eighteenth century.

The roof of the Doge's Palace covered with sheets of lead against the background of the Grand and Giudecca canals.

Bottom
De Pian, Room known as the Cameroto sotto piombo ("chamber under lead") where, by order of the State Inquisitors, the Capitano Grande went to read the death sentence.

Facing page, top left
*The Piombi had a less
forbidding atmosphere.
In fact, the seven small
rooms constructed
in the space under
the roof did not create
the same sense of total
and implacable isolation
as did the Pozzi or some*
*of the cells in the New
Prisons on the other side
of the canal. This current
view is comparable with
the descriptions
in the documents.*

*The torture chamber
in a seventeenth-century
drawing which shows
forms and objects closely
resembling the ones that
can be seen today.*

The Camera del Tormento

In the headquarters of the Signori di Notte al Criminal located in the block facing onto the basin there was a place known as the "Camera del Tormento" (torture chamber) because of the use to which it was put.

The Signori della Notte (Lords of the Night), a magistracy created around the middle of the thirteenth century to exercise justice, used the Camera del Tormento to try and sentence offenders who were guilty of uncommon but not very serious crimes. Thus the prisoners were interrogated in the same room in which, as was customary at the time, psychological and physical torture was carried out.

The lower part of the torture chamber. Against the rear wall was set the table of the magistrates who were present at torture sessions to hear any confessions by the unfortunate person suspended from the rope that can be seen in the

foreground. The large and deep space of the attic that opens onto the roof is visible above.

The torture chamber: upper passage with cells.

Facing page
The facade of the Prigioni Nuove on the other side of the canal has a particularly forceful structure: this conveys a sense of

monumentality in relation to the conceptual importance of the public building, while the severity of the architectural lines are an expression of its function, as seat of the Courts of Law and place of detention.

The Signori della Notte also had a preventive role, patrolling the city at night and making arrests. In addition they were obliged to meet in the palace immediately after the midday bell and remain there until sunset.

Up until 1558 this was the only torture chamber in the palace. Even those accused by the Council of Ten or the Inquisitors were brought to this room for interrogation and torture.

The place was much too open and great confusion reigned there, leading to protests from the Courts of Justice who called for greater secrecy. Consequently, the decision was taken to create a new torture chamber, in a space above the room of the Three Chiefs. The curator of the palace, Antonio da Ponte, had a short stretch of the pitched roof demolished and a large and well-lit garret built on the floor underneath: "...that I should see if there was room above the office of the Chiefs to accommodate the dar dela corda..."

"Dare di corda," or giving rope, was one of the methods of torture most widely practiced in Venice: perhaps the only one, apart from the lash. It entailed binding the prisoner's arms, from the wrists to the elbows, behind his back, raising him up and then breaking them by letting the weight of the body fall.

During the tour of the Secret Itineraries the chamber can be seen just as it was in those days, with all its furnishings: tables, chairs, cabinets and, in the middle, the rope hanging from a wooden pulley. A number of small cells had been created with wooden partitions nearby. These dark and suffocating rooms were used to hold prisoners, sometimes for long periods, before their interrogation and torture. This was a form of psychological pressure designed to make it easier to obtain confessions. The new "Tribunale del luogo della Corda" (Court of the place of the Rope), administered by the Ten, was more secret, harsh and severe than the older Camera del Tormento of the Signori della Notte.

The Prisons over the Canal

It is known that the space used to detain prisoners in the Doge's Palace was never either practical or sufficient to house all the inmates. Unsuccessful attempts to remedy the situation were made at various times, while the conditions in which the prisoners were kept grew increasingly precarious as time went by.

So the Republic considered the possibility of relocating the prisons outside the palace, and in particular in the existing structures on the

other side of the canal opposite the Renaissance flank of the palace.

The initiative was slow to get under way and at the beginning lacked a precise building program, with just a few rooms in an existing building being adapted.

The operation lasted for a century, despite the urgency and continuous pressure from the Council of Ten. By the middle of the sixteenth century, the Republic had decided to eliminate the prisons in the palace, except for the Pozzi and Piombi, and transfer all the prisoners to a new building on the other side of the canal.

A first design drawn up by Giovanni Rusconi was approved, but work was suspended when it was realized that the required improvements in conditions had not been provided for: the cells would have been even smaller and less well lit and ventilated than the original ones.

In 1569 further funding was approved to speed up the construction of the prison building.

The year of 1589 proved decisive to achieving a definitive solution to the problem. The commission of Provveditori appointed to deal with the matter instructed the curators of the palace to draw up complete plans for the building. It was to be laid out around an inner courtyard in the area comprised between the Riva and the monastery of Santa Scolastica, and between the canal and the Calle degli Albanesi.

Antonio da Ponte and Zamaria de' Piombi were entrusted with the project. They were assisted by a convict serving a life sentence, Zaccaria

Courtyard of the Prigioni Nuove on the other side of the canal. The design of the facades with the windows of the cells and the rooms used by the magistrates and the arched entrance is partially intended as an expression of the changes made to the legal system.

Portico of the Prigioni Nuove beyond the canal facing the Ponte della Paglia and the Doge's Palace.

Light and shadows of the Prigioni Nuove.

The room facing the basin side of the Prigioni Nuove, used for meetings of the Signori di Notte al Criminal.

Courtyard of the building of the Prigioni Nuove: grating in the north facade facing onto the church.

Window with iron bars of a cell in the prison on the outer patrol corridor.

Building of the Prigioni Nuove: walls and gratings facing onto the second courtyard.

Briani, whose suggestions earned him three years' remission to be spent in his own home.
The cost of the undertaking was calculated to be approximately 80,000 ducats.
The large rooms for the Signori di Notte al Criminal were to be located on the front facing onto the lagoon, on the second floor, while the rooms for the Inquisition, now demolished, would be situated at the rear. All the cells were grouped along the side of the building, on three floors. The plans provided for vaulted communal cells that were large in size and in particular with very high ceilings, and for rooms that were ventilated directly from the outside to be used for those called to make an "appearance." In 1589, in fact, the Council of Ten recommended that the work be continued and the necessary land, buildings and workshops be bought from their private owners, the Morosini and Foscari families. After being threatened with expropriation by the govern-

Jail in the Prigioni Nuove on the Calle degli Albanesi. The improvements that have been made are evident, with larger and higher cells and windows opening directly onto the outside.

Building of the Prigioni Nuove: a cell with a double grating.

*The windows of two cells
facing onto the Calle
degli Albanesi have bars
fixed to the wall with
screw bolts and two
wooden benches under
the grill. It appears that
prisoners could receive
visits from relatives and
friends here.*

Transverse patrol corridor of the cells on the second floor of the Prigioni Nuove set aside for use by the Council of Ten. They were built on the same principles as those used in the construction of the Pozzi. The work was halted by the government when it saw the discrepancy between the instructions given and the actual construction.

Corridor and cells of the Presentati (prisoners who had turned themselves in voluntarily) in the part of the building of the Prigioni Nuove facing onto the canal. The height of the door is sufficient in itself to demonstrate the different conditions of detention.

ment, they were induced to accept payments of 24,630 and 17,733 ducats respectively. Two public loans were also issued, for 10,000 and 25,000 ducats, at an interest ranging between 5 and 4.5 percent.

Many of the names used for the cells in the Doge's Palace were transferred to the rooms in the Prigioni Nuove (New Prisons). Their plan reveals the intention to improve the living conditions of the prisoners by providing larger, better lit and better ventilated cells.

At the same time a few sections, especially those under the control of the Council of Ten, offered conditions as harsh as those in the palace prisons.

Each cell was lined in the traditional manner, with crossed and heavily nailed planks of larch wood, fixed to the walls, floor and ceiling. While this lining protected the prisoner from the damp and from direct contact with the stone walls, it also became, especially in the summer, a breeding ground for all sorts of parasites and insects, such as bed bugs, cockroaches and fleas.

The exterior of the Prigioni Nuove presents a remarkable unity of architectural style, differing only in the marks that served to identify different functions. The reference is to the building facing onto the Riva with its ground-floor portico and large windows on the second floor with the alternating triangular and semi-circular projecting tympana that distinguish the seat of the Magistrati di Notte.

The massive blocks of Istrian stone from which the whole building is constructed underline its severity and security.

At the time in which they were built, the Prigioni Nuove were one of the earliest examples in Europe, if not the first, of an isolated single-block construction used as a State prison.

Antonio Contin and the Bridge of Sighs

On da Ponte's death in 1597, Antonio Contin, who had already supervised the construction

of the Prigioni Nuove, took over the position of curator of the palace, receiving more votes than any of his numerous rivals, including Scamozzi.

In 1600 Contin died and was succeeded by "Bortolo quondam Alessandro da Venetia," who was given the task of finishing what his predecessors had started and almost completed.

The Ponte dei Sospiri, or Bridge of Sighs, designed and begun by Contin to link the Pri-

The Bridge of Sighs seen from the back, looking toward San Giorgio of the basin.

The grill of Istrian stone in one of the windows of the Bridge of Sighs.

gioni Nuove with the Doge's Palace, was finished by Bortolo shortly before 1602.

The construction of this stone bridge, closed at the sides and roofed over, whose form and decoration show that Contin had already adopted the baroque manner, responded to a practical and functional need.

The structure, suspended above the canal and rendered highly expressive by the pattern of the blocks of Istrian stone and the lively and mixtilinear circular coping, is an extremely unusual feature. The interior of the bridge is split in two, with one passage leading to the Sala dei Censori and Sala dell'Avogaria and the other to the Sala del Mag-

The two parallel passages inside the Bridge of Sighs, viewed from the room into which it leads in the Prigioni Nuove. In the nineteenth century, the latter was freed of the group of cells that formed the fourth row on that floor.

The avogadori (lawyers) in the paintings that decorate the room in the palace on the other side of the canal can be seen at the back of the opening on the left.

istrato alle Leggi and Sala della Quarantia Criminal. The name "Bridge of Sighs" was assigned to it by nineteenth-century Romantic literature, during a time when it had practically ceased to be used for its original function.

Living Conditions of the Prisoners

The life of the inmates of the palace prisons was particularly harsh, difficult and at times brutal, especially in cells like the Pozzi belonging to the Council of the Ten.

The lack of light and air, the dampness of the walls, the frequently meager food, the dirt and stench, the impossibility of moving around in the overcrowded cells, the unbearable heat in the summer and freezing cold in the winter and the rats and parasites living under the wooden boards made these prisons, in mental and physical terms, a much heavier punishment than was intended by the sentences. In addition, the convicts often suffered from serious illnesses. The sanitary measures of the time and the inadequacy of medical knowledge certainly did not favor their recovery.

Another frequent cause of complaint and protest by the prisoners, in addition to the living conditions, was the behavior of the guards, their corruption and swindling over anything that was brought into the cells for payment.

However, these conditions were not the expression of a desire for excessive severity on the part of the judicial and prison authorities,

Facing page, bottom
The small room known as the parlatorio *("parlatory"). The stairs on the right lead to the Piombi, the ones on the left to the Bridge of Sighs.*

De Pian, Prisons called ovens in which those who did not want to admit their crimes were shut up, *engraving, Venice, Museo Correr. This image shows more clearly than any other the cruelty*

of the conditions in which prisoners were kept.

*A series of wooden doors
and gates subdivided the
patrol corridors, at least
in intention, into
various sectors based
on a classification of
the prisoners on the
basis of age, crime,
sentence and sex.
The photograph shows*
*all that is left of one
of the gates in the
women's ward.*

but the consequence of a widespread situation that derived, in the case of Venice, from the lack of space inside the palace, preventing the prisons from being laid out in a more functional manner.

The High Council, then the Senate and, from the fifteenth century onward, the Council of Ten had first-hand experience of the suffering of the inmates, but they were hardly ever capable of doing anything about it, in spite of the peremptory orders for an improvement or change in this lamentable situation. Until the radical decision was taken to build the Prigioni Nuove and abandon the ones in the palace.

The number of prisoners to be held in the various cells, laid down by the courts, was never adhered to because of the gulf between the shortage of space and the large number of prisoners. This was especially true in the sixteenth century, but was a problem in the seventeenth century as well. Both were periods in which there was a general decline in respect for and observance of laws in general and those governing prisons in particular.

The report by the physician Ottato in 1591 records conditions that were all too common. In fact he wrote that over ten convicts were held in the dark and dreadful Forte prisons when six could already have been considered

too many. And four of these ten prisoners were ill; as may be imagined, they caused considerable disturbance to the others.

An attempt was also made to vary the conditions of imprisonment in relation to the health of the convicts, and above all to the gravity of the crime: in fact prisoners could be assigned additional punishments such as fetters on the hands and feet, or given more lenient treatment by being placed in cells with windows opening directly onto the outside. They might also be permitted to keep their doors open in the daytime and walk in the corridors.

People who made an "appearance," i.e. turned themselves in when summonsed, were permitted a reduction in sentence, and even to be held in the courtyard of the palace, where they could move around freely and meet anyone they liked. At night they were able to rent rooms from the doge's stables to shelter from the cold and sleep. Others were granted release on parole during the day to work or attend to their affairs, as long as they returned to the prison at night.

A whole series of regulations serves to reflect and underline even more clearly, however indirectly, the degree of confusion within the prisons: murderers and thieves were not to be held in the same cell as debtors, prisoners awaiting trial were not to be shut up with those who had already been convicted and sentenced or, still worse, those condemned to death or imprisonment for life. The jailers were supposed to adhere scrupulously to the assignment of cells laid down in the sentence. They were also to prevent convicts moving from one prison to another and the entry of outsiders, people in masks, or women come "to gossip." Nor were female prisoners allowed to go into the cells of male prisoners, and vice versa. Finally the guards were not allowed to keep, even temporarily, the sums of money paid for the release of prisoners, but had to put them immediately in the coffers of the appropriate magistracy.

"PRESENTADI / LA CALINA": this was the name given to one of the cells of the Presentadi on the western part of the Prigioni Nuove on the other side of the canal.

The Petitions

The government of the Republic always paid a great deal of attention to petitions, not only the ones submitted by free citizens but also those of prisoners, debating them and voting on whether they should be accepted or rejected for true and just cause. The majority of requests made by prisoners turned on the possibility of obtaining some concession: a reduction in sentence, transfer to a cell with less harsh conditions for reasons of health or justice, protection against the avarice of the guards, a plea to provide for an abandoned and destitute family, and preferential treatment of all kinds in compensation for the most diverse services rendered to the Republic.

From the fifteenth century onward these pleas were heard by the Council of Ten and it was the practice to seek the opinion of the captain of the guards and, where illness was involved, the prison doctor.

The prisons most in demand in the requests for transfer appear to have been the Liona, Trona, Nuovissima, Giardini and Mocenigo, "...which are large and illuminated, and it will be greatly to the comfort of prisoners held in them, as the prisons of this city are very small and narrow..."

The guards and people responsible for surveillance were obliged to draw up reports and keep the Council of Ten, through the Chiefs, informed, even on a daily basis, of the overall situation in the prisons and the requests of the inmates themselves.

Sometimes, in particularly grave situations, an effort was made to assist the sick prisoner by moving him to more tolerable accommodation, even if it was used for other purposes: the living quarters of the captain of the Prigione Forte, the grooms' rooms or the courtyard, as we have already seen.

A payment of one or two thousand ducats could gain a prisoner temporary release or special assistance.

Along with this payment, which can be regarded as a sort of bail, Venetian justice also provided for the release of a prisoner by "pardon." Many convicts gained their freedom by this means at various times, as long as they had been given fairly light sentences or were in debt for modest sums.

Among the requests most frequently made in the petitions were those for some kind of assistance in the payment of the prison debts known as debts of justice, the agreement of terms with creditors, forms of payment by installment and permission to leave the prison to collect alms or deal with unfinished business. These were all measures designed to allow the convict to pay off his own debts, whether to the prison or to others, and gain his permanent release.

The petitions often made reference to the prisoner's family, to wives, children and parents left in dire poverty as a result of their relation's incarceration.

Another frequently made plea was from prisoners who had been jailed for a considerable period of time without undergoing trial: they asked for a decision to be made on their guilt or innocence.

Da Lorenzi, Monuments dedicated to the history of the Doge's Palace in Venice, *1868: petition from a group of Slavonians living in Venice on behalf of their imprisoned and indigent fellow countrymen.*

Petitions were submitted by fugitives and exiles. Many people complained of abuses and swindles carried out by the guards and their captains.

Finally, it was requested that a sentence, passed in too cursory a fashion by minor courts, be revised by the Council of Ten so that "justice" be done in a fairer and more credible way. When defendants were acquitted, the court used to grant them modest sums of money as compensation. Sometimes the home of a person held in custody was recognized as a place of imprisonment, a practice corresponding to the modern one of house arrest.

It was with the creation of the Council of Ten, in 1310, as well as those of the Three Chiefs and the Inquisitors, that laws began to be applied to the prison institution with greater consistency, although its overall functioning never matched the decisions that were taken.

In addition to the institutions already mentioned, in fact, the Magistrati al Criminal (Criminal Justices), Cinque Anziani alla Pace (Five Elders for Peace), Auditori Vecchi e Nuovi (Old and New Auditors), Avogadri (Advocates) and others were invested with respon-

The Hall of the Three Chiefs.

sibilities in judicial matters and this subdivision of competence had created considerable confusion in the way the prisons were run.

Bread

Prisoners were entitled, if declared needy, to a free ration of bread. The confraternities also provided large amounts of bread, considered an essential and indispensable food, the basis of the convict's diet. The Republic called for public tenders for the daily supply of bread. It has to be said, however, that, in spite of all their efforts, the authorities were never able to obtain a product whose weight and quality corresponded to what had been requested and paid for. The suppliers always found some way to produce lower-quality bread than was called for in the specifications or to cheat on the weight.

The bakers who won contracts were inspected daily by a representative of the Rason Vecchie, but a combination of mutual backscratching and the habit of swindling the Republic, in this case at the expense of the prisoners, meant that the watchdogs and the watched always came to an agreement. Around 1620 the Council decided to entrust this task to the Fraterna di San Bartolomeo. Later responsibility for inspection was given back to the Rason Vecchie, with the issuing of contracts with more detailed terms and the application of stiffer penalties against those who broke them.

Each prisoner was entitled to two nine-ounce loaves of bread a day, equivalent to over half a kilo of "... leavened bread, well-cooked ..." inside and out.

In 1709 fresh bread was replaced by biscuits. While these were much less nutritious, it was easier to control their quality and weight. Convicts often sold them or used them for barter.

The Advocate

To insure that all the orders issued on behalf of prisoners by the High Council and the Council of Ten were carried out, the post of the Official

Advocate was created. He was required go at least once a month, both before and after the proceedings, to visit the infirmary and the communal cells, check on the activities of the whole guard service and, after appraising the truthfulness and validity of the charges, present written reports to the Avogadori. The advocate was free to enter any cell to listen to prisoners and question them about their legal cases, living conditions and state of health.

The advocate also functioned as a defense lawyer before the Council of Ten. The large amount of work this entailed led to the appointment of a second advocate.

So the advocate for poverty-stricken convicts was another of those institutions set up to help the prison population. Yet the institution was very unsatisfactory owing to the partiality of the interventions and the two office holders' lack of legal knowledge. In the eighteenth century an attempt was made to remedy this by appointing only jurists of recognized ability, with the title of Criminal Procurator, to check, supervise and advise the two advocates.

The Infirmaries and the Doctor

In the sixteenth century the already unhealthy palace prisons became even more so as a consequence of the large numbers of people detained in them. Many of them were sick and their diseases were often infectious.

The greatest problems were encountered during the summer season, with a marked increase in the death rate.

In addition, it was quickly realized that the

Advocate and Public Prosecutor, *from Jan Grevembroch,* Gli abiti dè veneziani, *Venice, Museo Correr.*

sick, even when moved to less uncomfortable cells, were the cause of great difficulties and disturbance for the healthy prisoners with whom they were housed, owing to their inability to look after themselves.

These and other considerations led to rooms being set aside for the ill, the so-called "infirmaries." They were located inside the prisons, but offered milder and healthier conditions and where possible were illuminated and ventilated from the outside. In the old palace prisons, the Schiava cells of the Forte group, the Cameroto of the Nuovissime, the Malpaga above the Liona and several others including the Moceniga were used for this purpose.

Resembling the infirmaries found in monasteries, they were furnished with trestles, wooden bedsteads, mattresses, sheets and blankets. These were sometimes supplied to the poor by the State, but more often by the Fraterne.

For a long time these innovations were held back not just by the habits of the past, but also by the inability to organize matters, as a result of too many assignments to different courts with varying degrees of importance.

In the middle of the eighteenth century the existing infirmaries were supplemented by two new ones in the Prigioni Nuove. The first was reserved for women, the second for those serving life sentences.

The assistance provided to convicts by the Republic extended to medical treatment as well. The doctor helped the sick but was also responsible for checking abuses and detecting malingering. Chosen from among the most capable in the city, the physician was obliged to examine the sick and give his opinion of the gravity of the illness in his diagnosis, written under oath. He was to issue instructions for immediate treatment and keep the Avogadori di Comune informed of the course taken by the illness and the eventual recovery. After 1564, it was the College of Physicians that elected one of its own members to the post. The medicines prescribed were bought in the city's pharmacies and given to patients by the guards. The medicines were paid for by the patient himself, if he was capable of doing so. Otherwise the government took the required sums from the prisoners' funds, which were managed by the Avogadori. The diagnoses were very empirical and give a clear idea of the limitations of medical knowledge at the time.

The most common illnesses affected the respiratory system or gastrointestinal tract, and therefore included typhoid fevers and spasms. Ringworm, scabies, sores, gangrene, epilepsy, syphilis, insanity and manic depression were also widespread.

The Confraternities

Throughout the centuries of the Republic's existence there were numerous confraternities or welfare societies of citizens in Venice that took care of the needs of prisoners, especially the indigent ones, often keeping them alive.

The Fraterne, as they were called, often took the place of the State, which did no more than provide a bed, some blankets and, in cases of extreme poverty, modest sums of money. The main aim of the Fraterne was to collect alms to contribute to the payment of the convict's legal debts, i.e. the expenses incurred for detention, release, trial and damages to third parties. Prisoners received assistance not only from the Fraterne, but also from the Scuole and Corporazioni delle Arti, from private citizens, and from the churches, where money was collected for them during religious services.

It was in the fifteenth century that the initia-

Doctor, *from Jan Grevembroch,* Gli abiti dè veneziani, *Venice, Museo Correr.*

La Confraternità deputata alla Giustitia, che accompagna i Giustitiati della Città di Venetia, il cui habito e un sacco di tela negra, lungo fin terra, con un capuccio col qual loro si coprano la faccia.

tives on behalf of prisoners began to be organized around associations that assumed a permanent character, regulated by written statutes.

The confraternities administered the parts of testaments that concerned prisoners.

Each member paid a fixed sum toward the release or assistance of other members who had fallen foul of the law.

This assistance was extended to the needy families of prisoners.

The Fraterne made purchases and exercised control over the quality and control of the food, especially bread, which had to be fresh and well-baked, as well as soup, meat, water and wine. When wine was bought by private individuals for prisoners, the Republic waived the duty on the purchase.

When carrying out this assistance work, members of the confraternity were granted the right to make frequent visits to the convicts in their cells or in places set aside for interviews, in order to hear their complaints and requests, as well as to see what their most urgent needs were at first hand. The assemblies of the Fraterne had been open to the public from the outset and were attended by the relatives and friends of the prisoner to plead his cause and to press for concrete financial aid that would resolve the problem. A graded list was drawn up for the most needy prisoners, based on such factors as their relative youth, state of health, type of sentence and gravity of the crime, and the kind of life they had led before incarceration. From the start the Republic regarded the initiatives of the Fraterne as a valid complement to those of a public character; indeed the privatization of assistance presented many advantages, as it was the expression of a genuine desire to attend to real needs. The most important element in the organization of the Fraterne and in the implementation of the programs on behalf of prisoners was the raising of money to pay debts and obtain their release. A document known as a "fede" (faith or certificate) was drawn up, bearing the emblem of the confraternity and giving the name of the prisoner and the sum required for his release. The fede was circulated in the city in order to raise subscriptions toward the sum indicated. When this was reached, the Fraterna paid off the debt and the prisoner was able to regain his freedom.

Sentencing to the Galleys and the Death Penalty

In the sixteenth century Venice decided for the first time to send convicts to row ships as an alternative to incarceration, a system that had been in use for some time in other European states. The delay in the use of criminals on the galleys can be explained by the Republic's attitude toward its merchant fleet and navy. Its strength and wealth were founded on shipping, which allowed it to carry out trade and establish naval bases along the coasts of the Adriatic and the eastern Mediterranean. So there was a reluctance to rely on convicts to man the galleys, which the Venetians saw as a mobile part of the lagoon

The Confraternity representing Justice that parades executed men through the City of Venice, who are dressed in a habit of black cloth, reaching to the ground and with a hood that they use to cover their faces, *from Vecellio*, Habiti d'Italia, *Venice, Museo Correr.*

Convict, *from Jan Grevembroch*, Gli abiti dè veneziani, *Venice, Museo Correr.*

Facing page, top *Giacomo Franco*, Prison exercise in the square, *engraving, Venice, Doge's Palace.*

Facing page, bottom *Galeazza, engraving.*

L'Ecc.mo G.nale mette à banco le Galere doue si fà vn Solen.mo apparato si Zop= zarie et, si mette fuori gran quantità di Tapeti d'oro et, argenti et in particolare vna Cassona di Verghe d'oro di valuta d'vn Millione ... &c

city. When the idea was finally accepted it was with the threefold aim, as was pointed out by the Council of Ten itself, of reducing the overcrowding in the palace prisons, making up the shortfall in free oarsmen and reducing the cost of manning the galleys.

It was also considered to have a social aspect: the reeducation of the convict took place much more rapidly through his active participation, even if chained to an oar, in the life of the city than through inactive detention in prison, which undermined both the body and the mind. A year at the oar of a galley was worth two in prison.

The Venetian system of justice also provided for the death penalty, which remained in force throughout the Republic's existence, though toward the end it was applied less and less frequently. Executions were either carried out secretly in the cells, by strangulation, or in public, by hanging or beheading between the two columns known as Marco and Todaro in the Piazzetta. The corpses were sometimes put on display between the red columns of the palace loggia. The text and motivations of all death sentences were posted up in the Sala del Maggior Consiglio. Some of them, as a warning to

GALEAZZE
(Vedute per Poppa, e per franco
Dedicate
All' Illustrissimo, et Eccellentissimo Signore Angelo Emo, Patritio Veneto,
Gouernatore di Galeazza per la Serenissima Republica

all, were made known to the citizens by proclamation in St. Mark's Square and at Rialto.

After execution, the body was sometimes left on the gallows for periods of varying length, to serve as an example to the people.

The texts of the death sentences were extremely short and concise and over the course of the centuries not many changes were made in the provisions governing executions. The Gastaldo, or Chamberlain, was in charge of the operation. Sometimes part of the prisoner's body was amputated prior to his execution,

generally the right hand, tongue or an ear. This cruel practice of mutilation undoubtedly had a symbolic significance for Venetian justice and was related in some way to the crime committed. This is confirmed by the fact that the amputated part was hung around the neck of the condemned man.

Visits to the Prisons

After arrest, no prisoner was allowed contact with anyone apart from the lawyer who would defend him at the trial. In fact the prisoner, once interrogated, did not even have the right to be present at his trial, let alone speak on his own behalf. The prohibition on communication with anyone, equivalent to the modern practice of solitary confinement, was intended to prevent tampering with the evidence, but was supposed to continue even after the trial. However, there are many documents showing that this was not enforced. In fact this regulation, which was supposed to apply to everyone, was subject to many exceptions, such as the nominal permits issued by the High Council, the visits by Fraterne and the frequent contacts between convicts and relatives, friends and benefactors. Even the inmates of the prisons of the Council of Ten, generally considered a threat to the security of the State and kept under close guard, were able to meet and communicate with people who were not part of the machinery of the State, such as agents for business dealings that were underway or to be undertaken: "... that in the future any of the prisoners, who want to speak with his relatives or agents ... should be allowed to hold this discussion in the chamber at the foot of the stairs..." This was a room with a small barred window through which the prisoner could speak with visitors.

In the eighteenth century the Avogadori di Comun tried, without success, to regulate visits by women to the infirmaries, but the problem extended to all the other prisons as well.

Women visiting inmates, whether they were wives, daughters or other relatives, had to have a permit bearing the precise name of the prisoner and the degree of their relationship. Relations between prisoners and prostitutes constituted another problem for the Council, which was unable, or perhaps unwilling, ever to solve it. The guards were bribed to make such visits possible.

In 1627 the Council of Ten expressed its disapproval of the fact that women from outside, whether wives, lovers or whores, were being allowed into the prison and spending the night there with the illicit complicity of the guards.

In addition, the law strictly prohibited prisoners from sending or receiving messages without prior censorship by the State. But here too, given the total confusion and widespread corruption, prisoners found ways round such rules. In fact it was inconceivable that the prison regulations imposed by the Ten would be respected under such conditions of structural decay and with prisons that communicated directly with the outside, under the porticoes or along the canal.

Lighting

The records concerning the oil lamps that the inmates kept burning day and night contain many contradictions. The danger of fire was a constant concern for the government, which greatly feared its consequences. Whence the aforementioned contradictions, for it proved impossible to totally prohibit the comfort offered by light, however dim.

The oil for these lamps was almost always bought

Facing page, top
Da Pian, Camerotto detto Giardin Scuro ("cell known as the dark garden") where prisoners were strangled on the orders of what was then the Council of Ten, *engraving, Venice, Museo Correr.*

Facing page, bottom
View of the loggia overlooking the Piazzetta of the Doge's palace: two columns are of red marble.

Courtesan, *from Jan Grevembroch,* Gli abiti dè veneziani, *Venice, Museo Correr.*

from private citizens or provided by the Fraterne, who also made sure it was fairly distributed among the cells.

While lamps were not prohibited, efforts were made to avert the danger by eliminating cells scattered around the palace and grouping others together in places of great safety. In 1525 the rooms used as prisons above and below the Avogaria Vecchia and Nuova and near the Sala della Bolla were emptied of their occupants. Seven years later and for the same reason (there had been an outbreak of fire which had fortunately been brought under control),

almost all the cells in Torresella were eliminated, with the demolition of their wooden linings and partitions. Where it proved impossible to move the cells, steps were taken to isolate them from adjoining rooms by the construction of brick walls and vaults.

The Prison Guards

The prisons were controlled by guards under the command of a captain, divided into different groups responsible for various types of cells and answering to the orders of various magistracies.

Anonymous, The Doge's
Palace on Fire in 1577.

The inadequacy of the guard service, one of the principal causes of the disorganized state of the prisons, can be deduced today from the innumerable petitions submitted by prisoners in which they claimed to have been cheated or unjustly persecuted as a result of the unchecked use of power on the part of the guards. Bribes, tolls, demands for money, the purloining of food, drink or clothing, and the exorbitance of the charges made for any kind of service rendered to the prisoners were everyday practices, methodically and constantly applied. The phenomenon became the dishonest go-between, not just within the prison but from the inside to the outside and vice versa, that had to be used by both prisoners and suppliers.

In addition the ambiguity of the attitude shown by the State, which passed all sorts of specific laws designed to punish abuses but never made any determined attempt to apply them, gave it even more space in which to grow. The greed and dishonesty of the guards, and perhaps of the whole system for control of the prisons, went unpunished and no attempt was made at concealment, in the certainty that nothing would be done.

All this in spite of the fact the Council of Ten had held a series of inquiries and checks, as well as increasing the penalties.

In general the guards were paid very little, as if on the tacit assumption that illicit proceeds and so-called perks would make up the greater part of their earnings.

Escapes

The security and efficiency of the Republic's prisons were continuously put to the test by their inmates, who with infinite patience dug, broke and sawed their way through floors, walls, doors and window bars, or quickly and

Capitano Grande, *from Jan Grevembroch,* Gli abiti dè veneziani, *Venice, Museo Correr.*

boldly took advantage of events to make a dash for freedom. On occasion these escape bids succeeded, but most of them were foiled.

The negligence of the guards, the confusion that reigned in all the prisons, the difficulty of maintaining an effective surveillance owing to the small number of jailers and the complex layout of the structures and the parlous state of the walls and floors sometimes permitted these attempts to come off, especially in the prisons in the palace. With the construction of the Prigioni Nuove on the other side of the canal, however, escapes became much less frequent. Numerous surviving documents give us an idea of the frequency, manner and location of the escapes that were made at various times, in particular from the palace prisons.

In 1397 many prisoners escaped from the Camera di Tormento of the Signori di Notte, taking advantage of the inadequate security of the cells and the inefficiency of the guards.

Following a series of such escapes the Council of Ten decided to wall up the windows, turning the cells into extremely harsh environments.

So many cases of sickness and death resulted from this measure that the windows were reopened again after some time.

Restoration work was continually being carried out in all the cells, either to repair damage or to make them more secure.

Escape bids were even made from the prisons within the competence of the Council of Ten, with the exception of the Pozzi, notwithstanding the higher level of surveillance and stricter control.

In an attempt to foil the frequent escapes, inspections were carried out without warning in the daytime and even at night. The convicts' possessions were searched for tools or implements that could be used to make holes in the walls, smuggled into the prisons by accomplices or relatives.

In 1507, 1510 and 1540 numerous cells were re-

The first cell of the Piombi in which Casanova was held at the beginning of his detention and from which he made his first attempt to escape, by breaking through the wooden floor under the roof.

One of the eastern rooms of the Piombi which used to house two adjoining cells. It was from one of these that Casanova made his second, and successful, escape bid.

paired after breakouts by prisoners. Under such circumstances the guards themselves were subject to investigations, though these hardly ever reached any conclusions.

There was a breakout from the Schiava prison in 1546, and from the one called Strombolo in 1548.

Two more attempts in those years were discovered before the prisoners could escape.

In 1551 repairs had to be made to the Liona and Malpaga prisons. In 1561 the bars on a window were sawed through and in 1564 the wall of the Forte prison, underneath that of the Tribunale in the Sala del Maggior Consiglio, was repaired after the damage caused to it by tunneling on the ground floor.

When the famous fire that destroyed that room broke out in 1577, it was blamed for the damage. But the causes were quite different, as the curator da Ponte pointed out. And so we could go on for a long time listing the escapes that were made or the discovery of the numerous cases of broken walls and floors "...made by prisoners with violence and with intelligence too..."

The penalty for escape was the addition of a number of years to the sentence to be served. In reality the punishments inflicted for escaping, while varying from period to period, were never very severe, so long as the convict had not committed any other serious crimes during his attempt at flight. It appears that the Republic admitted the theoretical right of the prisoner to try to escape from incarceration even by unlawful means, just as the courts attempted, by application of the law, to keep them in their cells until their sentences had been served.

In 1463 the penalty was set at one year of imprisonment and the payment of any reward due to the discover of the escape bid. Later, as damage to the prisons increased, so did the penalties, rising as high as six years or exile.

One of the most celebrated escapes was the one made on October 31, 1756, by Giacomo Casanova. He described his daring flight in a book that was read all over Europe and helped to establish his reputation as an adventurous and courageous man.

Giacomo Casanova's second and successful attempt to escape from the cells of the Piombi with aid of his father Balbi (from Giacomo Casanova, Histoire de ma fuite).

Photograph Credits
Archivio Electa, Milan
Archivio Palazzo Ducale, Venice
Any person claiming to hold copyright
for illustrations that have not been identified
should contact the publisher

This book was printed for Mondadori Electa S.p.A.
at Mondadori Printing S.p.A., Via Castellana 98,
Martellago (Venice) in the year 2004